Disney · PIXAR

COCO

The Story of Dante

Level 1

T0345665

Re-told by: Louise Fonceca
Series Editor: Rachel Wilson

Before You Read

In This Book

Dante   Miguel   Grandmother

Activity

Read and say.

1 Dante is a ...
  a cat
  b dog

2 Dante is ...
  a happy
  b sad

This is Dante.
He has brown eyes and big ears.

He gets food from a garden.
He drinks some water.

There are no friends here.
Dante runs and runs.

Dante sees cats and dogs.
They play. He is happy.

Dante is hungry. He smells food.
Mmmmm. Where is it?

This is the town.
Good! There's some food here.

Dante sees a nice boy.
He's Miguel. Hello, dog!

There are some nice people in the town.
Here's some bread. *Woof!*

Here's some meat.
Dante likes meat. *Woof!*

This is the teacher.
Here's some water. *Woof!*

Dante is hungry again.
Bad dog! *Shoo!*
Dante runs from Grandmother.

Dante is sad. Where is Miguel?
He likes Miguel.

Here he is! Miguel plays the guitar.
Dante listens.

Dante has a friend.
And Miguel has a pet!

After You Read

1 **What happens first, second, and third?**

2 **Read and say Yes or No.**

1 Dante likes food.

2 There is some food in the town.

3 Dante eats bread and meat.

4 Miguel is a nice boy.

5 The teacher gives some bread to Dante.

6 Grandmother likes Dante.

Picture Dictionary

bread

food

friends

guitar

meat

people

smell

town

water

Phonics

Say the sounds. Read the words.

C c

cake

cat

G g

garden

girl

Say the rhyme.

In the garden, there's a cat.
There's a girl in a hat.
In the garden, there's a boat.
There's a girl in a coat.

Values

Stay positive.

What foods are healthy?

Healthy food is good for you.
Fruit and vegetables are healthy food.
Chocolate and cakes are nice for a treat.

It's a party!

bread · butter · cake · chocolate · cheese

fish · french fries · fruit · vegetables

What's for dinner?

Pearson Education Limited
KAO Two
KAO Park, Harlow,
Essex, CM17 9NA, England
and Associated Companies throughout the world.

ISBN: 978-1-2923-4666-3

This edition first published by Pearson Education Ltd 2020

9 10 8

Set in Heinemann Roman Special, 19pt/28pt
Printed and bound in Great Britain by Bell & Bain Ltd, Glasgow

Published by Pearson Education Limited

Acknowledgments
123RF.com: eivaisla 21, Natthapon Ngamnithiporn 21, Richard Griffin 21, Vassiliy Prikhodko 21
Getty Images: YangYin 17
Shutterstock.com: 81593 21, Africa Studio 21, Elena Larina 18, ESB Professional 18, holbox 16, LedyX 17, Lopolo 20, New Africa 21, noophoto 21, Rob Byron 21, wavebreakmedia 21

For a complete list of the titles available in the Pearson English Readers series, visit www.pearsonenglishreaders.com.

Alternatively, write to your local Pearson Education office or to Pearson English Readers Marketing Department, Pearson Education, KAO Two, KAO Park, Harlow, Essex, CM17 9NA